They Just Know
Animal Instincts

by Robin Yardi

illustrated by Laurie Allen Klein

No one reminds a caterpillar to eat her leaves, or to make a chrysalis when she's old enough. Caterpillars just know.

When a newly-hatched butterfly takes her first flight, she doesn't need anyone to hold her gently by the wing. Butterflies just know.

Mother butterflies lay their eggs on a tasty plant and fly away.

New caterpillars and butterflies just know what to do, all on their own!

Nobody tells a horn shark to stay in the shallow end until he can swim.

When it gets dark, no one leaves a light on in the deep, dark sea so he won't get scared.

When he's hungry, the baby shark doesn't eat gooey baby food. But he doesn't need to wait for his teeth to come in, either.

Mother horn sharks lay their eggs and swim away.

New horn sharks just know how to swim, all on their own.

No one makes sure a little ladybug wears a helmet while her shell changes color and hardens.

No one teaches her to make a wish when she is blown away on a dandelion puff.

When she does fly away on the warm summer wind, red and black against the blue sky, nobody needs to take a picture.

Mother ladybugs lay their eggs and fly away.

Ladybug larvae just know what to do, all on their own.

Nobody takes tiny spring peeper tadpoles to school.
When their little legs come in, no one gives them
leaping lessons.

When it's time to sing in the spring, they all know the same tinkling song, and they all sing along.

Mother peepers lay a lot of lovely eggs and hop away. Little tadpoles just know what to do, all on their own.

No one rocks sea turtle hatchlings to sleep, or sings a soft song all night long.

When baby turtles swim across the sea, they don't need to hold flippers and wait for ocean current lights to change. They just know where to go, what to do, and how to cross the ocean blue.

Mother sea turtles dig a deep hole in warm soft sand, lay their eggs, and then swim away.

Turtle hatchlings just know what to do, all on their own.

No one teaches baby kingsnakes that biting isn't a good way to make friends.

And kingsnakes don't shop for long pants when they are ready to shed their old skin.

When they go to bed, baby kingsnakes definitely don't need stuffed animals to squeeze. They already are stuffed with animals.

Mother kingsnakes lay a clutch of eggs in a secret spot and slither away.

New kingsnakes just know how
to hunt and shed their skin as
they grow, all on their own.

Butterflies just know how to fly.

Little horn sharks just know how to swim.

Baby sea turtles just know where to go.

Ladybug larvae just know how to find all the aphids they want.

Little spring peepers just know how to sing their songs.

And kingsnakes just know how to grow all on their own. They don't need toys, or help, or hugs . . .

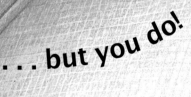

. . . but you do!

For Creative Minds

Instinct versus Learned Behaviors

Animals do some things without even thinking about it. These behaviors, called instinct, help animals live in their habitats. These behaviors come naturally to the animals and all animals of the same type will do them without being taught.

For example, if you have a baby brother or sister, you'll see that the baby cries when hungry and laughs or smiles when happy. Other examples of instinctual behavior include birds building nests, turtles (cold-blooded reptiles) basking in the sun to warm up, and skinks breaking off their tails to escape predators.

Many animals are born without ever knowing their parents. They don't have anyone to teach them how to find food or how to survive—they survive purely on instinct. These behaviors are inherited from parents, even if the animals never know their parents. Any behavior that is not learned is considered instinct.

Most mammal and bird parents raise their young. Adults teach so that the young learn how to do things. Young humans learn to read, ride bikes, and write. Young birds learn to fly. Young wolves learn to hunt for food.

Some behaviors are a combination of instinct and things they learn. For example, between 6 and 9 months old, human babies instinctually start to babble to communicate. Their parents will teach them a language, like English or Spanish.

Sometimes animals learn things by observing other animals or by figuring something out. A young bear might learn where to go to find juicy berries. Eagles may figure out that salmon swim upstream at certain times of year and are easy to catch. A young human might learn that it's easier to make friends by being nice than by being mean.

What are some things that you have learned how to do? Who taught you or how did you figure it out?

Identify which behaviors are instinct and which are learned.
Can you explain why?

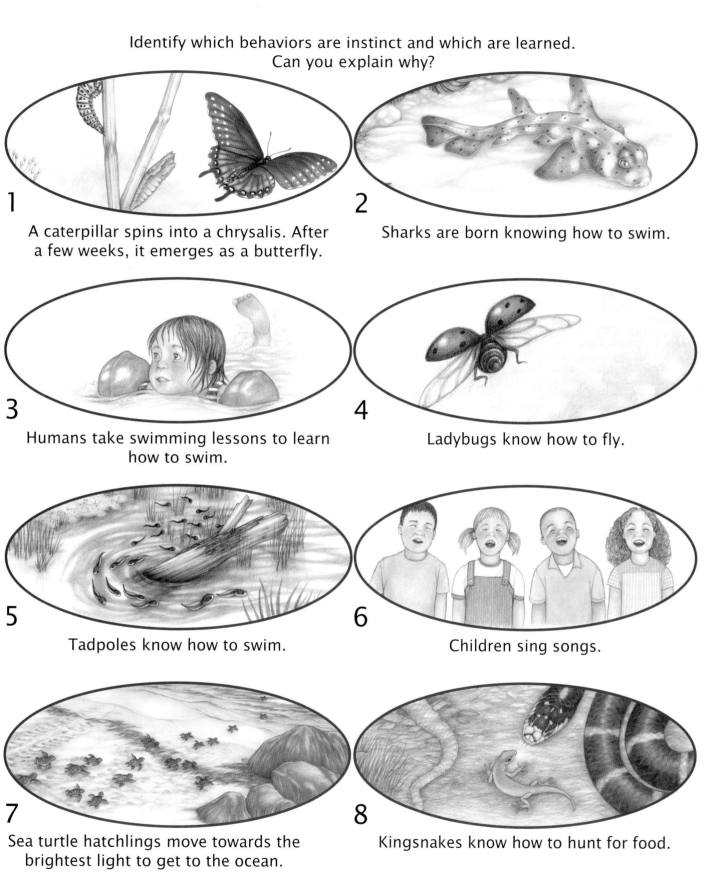

1 A caterpillar spins into a chrysalis. After a few weeks, it emerges as a butterfly.

2 Sharks are born knowing how to swim.

3 Humans take swimming lessons to learn how to swim.

4 Ladybugs know how to fly.

5 Tadpoles know how to swim.

6 Children sing songs.

7 Sea turtle hatchlings move towards the brightest light to get to the ocean.

8 Kingsnakes know how to hunt for food.

Instinct: 1, 2, 4, 5, 7, 8   Learned Behavior: 3, 6

Young and Their Parents

Some young animals look like small versions of the adults they will become. Other young look very different from adults. They may undergo a complete change as part of their life cycle, their eye color might change, or the color of their fur or feathers might change as they get older. Can you match the young (numbers) to the adult animals (letters)?

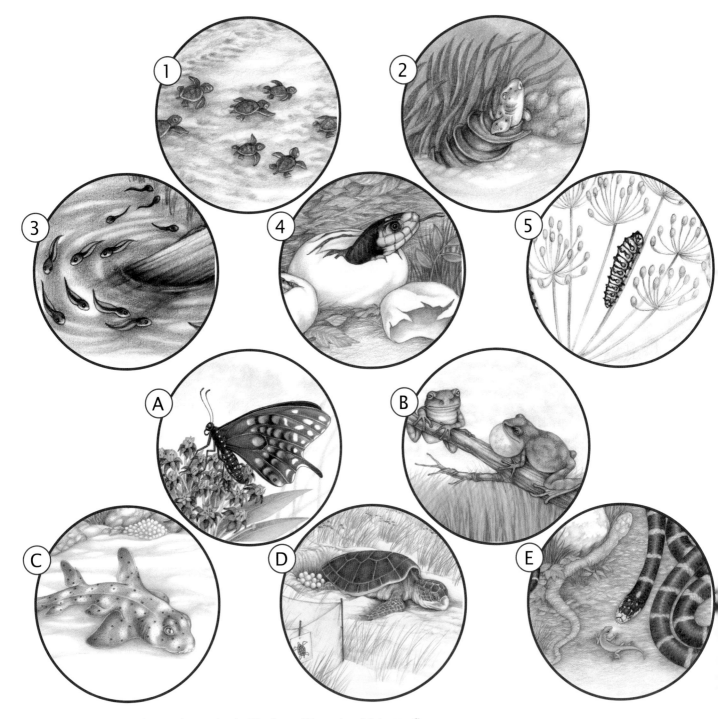

Answers: 1D: sea turtle, 2C: horn shark, 3B: frog, 4E: snake, 5A butterfly

Life Cycles: Metamorphosis

All living things have life cycles. Plants grow from seeds. Animals are born or hatch and grow into adults. Some animals go through a complete change, called metamorphosis, from the time they hatch or are born to what they eventually look like as adults. Butterflies, frogs and ladybugs all undergo a complete metamorphosis.

- Eggs hatch into larvae that don't look anything like the adults.
- The larvae eat, grow, and molt. When they are grown, they turn into pupae.
- The pupa stage is a time of change.
- Adult insects emerge from pupae.
- The adults lay eggs to start the process all over again.

Can you find some life-cycle changes in the illustrations?

adult frog

adult frogs

egg mass

tadpoles

tadpoles with legs

young frogs

A butterfly's pupa is called a chrysalis.

pupa

adult

larva

egg

pupa

larva

eggs

After the pupa stage, a ladybug's shell hardens and changes color.

adult

For all our little ones, who will learn to do so much!—RY
To BK and JK, through every stage and transition, thank you for sharing every adventure—LAK
Thanks to Dr. Carrie Kappel, conservation biologist and former youth educator at the Teton Science Schools, for reviewing the accuracy of the information in this book.

The author donates a portion of her royalties to Wilderness Youth Project (wyp.org).

Library of Congress Cataloging-in-Publication Data

Yardi, Robin, author.
  They just know : animal instincts / by Robin Yardi ; illustrated by Laurie Allen Klein.
    pages cm
  Audience: Ages 4-8
  ISBN 978-1-62855-634-6 (english hardcover) -- ISBN 978-1-62855-639-1 (english pbk.) -- ISBN 978-1-62855-649-0 (english downloadable ebook) -- ISBN 978-1-62855-659-9 (english interactive dual-language ebook) -- ISBN 978-1-62855-644-5 (spanish pbk.) -- ISBN 978-1-62855-654-4 (spanish downloadable ebook) -- ISBN 978-1-62855-664-3 (spanish interactive dual-language ebook) 1. Instinct--Juvenile literature. 2. Animal behavior--Juvenile literature. 3. Adaptation (Biology)--Juvenile literature. I. Klein, Laurie Allen, illustrator. II. Title.
  QL781.Y37 2015
  591.5'12--dc23
                            2015009001

Translated into Spanish: *¡Ellos ya saben! Instintos de los animales*

Lexile® Level: AD 870L
key phrases for educators: animal life cycles, instinct versus learned behaviors

Bibliography:

The Audubon Society Pocket Guide to Familiar Insects and Spiders of North America. New York: Knopf, 1988. Print.
"California Kingsnake - Lampropeltis Californiae." California Kingsnake. N.p., n.d. Web. 03 Mar. 2015.
Carter, David J., and Frank Greenaway. Butterflies and Moths. New York: Dorling Kindersley, 1992. Print.
"Critter Catalog." BioKIDS. University of Michigan, n.d. Web. 03 Mar. 2015.
Evans, Arthur V., and James N. Hogue. Introduction to California Beetles. Berkeley: U of California, 2004. Print.
"Horn Shark." , Kelp Forest, Fishes, Heterodontus Francisci at the Monterey Bay Aquarium. N.p., n.d. Web. 03 Mar. 2015.
"Ladybugs, Ladybug Pictures, Ladybug Facts - National Geographic." National Geographic. N.p., n.d. Web. 03 Mar. 2015.
"Loggerhead Sea Turtle - National Wildlife Federation." Loggerhead Sea Turtle - National Wildlife Federation. N.p., n.d. Web. 07 Apr. 2015.
O'Shea, Mark, and Tim Halliday. Reptiles and Amphibians. New York: DK Pub., 2001. Print.
Scott, James A. The Butterflies of North America: A Natural History and Field Guide. Stanford, CA: Stanford UP, 1986. Print.

Manufactured in China, June 2015
This product conforms to CPSIA 2008
First Printing

Arbordale Publishing
Mt. Pleasant, SC 29464
www.ArbordalePublishing.com